The Art
of
Painting
on
Silk

Volume 2
Soft Furnishings

Other books published by Search Press

Beginner's Guide to Silk Painting *by Mandy Southan*

A Complete Guide to Silk Painting *by Susanne Hahn*

The Art of Painting on Silk Volume 1 *edited by Pam Dawson*

The Art of Painting on Silk Volume 2 *– Soft Furnishings, edited by Pam Dawson*

The Art of Painting on Silk Volume 3 *– Fashions, edited by Pam Dawson*

The Art of Painting on Silk Volume 4 *– Potpourri, edited by Pam Dawson*

Inspirational Silk Painting from Nature *by Renate Henge*

Introduction to Batik *by Margaret Horne & Heather Griffin*

Marbling on Fabric *by Anne Chambers*

Paint Your Own T Shirts *by Monika Neubacher-Fesser & Deiter Köhnen*

The Art
of
Painting
on
Silk

Volume 2
Soft Furnishings

Edited by Pam Dawson

Search Press

Acknowledgements

First published in Great Britain 1988
Search Press Ltd
Wellwood, North Farm Road,
Tunbridge Wells, Kent TN2 3DR

Reprinted 1989, 1991, 1994, 1998

This book has been rewritten and rearranged from
original French editions of *Peinture Sur Soie* copyright ©
Les Editions de Saxe-Peinture sur Soie 1985, 1986, 1897

English version *The Art of Painting on Silk Volume 2 – Soft
Furnishings* copyright © Search Press Limited 1988

Translated by Paul Burns

Our thanks to Pongees Limited of London, wholesale
Importers of Silk, for the information shown on page 10.

ISBN 0 85532 623 9

Phototypeset by Scribe Design, Gillingham, Kent
Printed in Spain by Elkar S. Coop, Bilbao

Converting centimetres to inches	
centimetres	*inches*
1.25	½
2	¾
2.5	1
3	1¼
3.5	1⅜
4	1½
4.5	1¾
5	2
5.5	2⅛
6	2¼

If readers have difficulty obtaining any of the materials or equipment mentioned in this book,
please write for further information to the publishers. If you are interested in any of the art and craft
titles published by Search Press, then please send for a free colour catalogue to:

Search Press Ltd.,
Department B,
Wellwood, North Farm Road, Tunbridge Wells,
Kent TN2 3DR, England
Tel: (01892) 510850   Fax: (01892) 515903
E-mail: sales@searchpress.com

or (if resident in the USA) to:
Arthur Schwartz & Co., Inc,
234 Meads Mountain Road,
Woodstock, NY 12498
Tel: (914) 679 4024   Fax: (914) 679 4093
Orders, toll-free: 800 669 9080

CONTENTS

Introduction and how to begin

Silk has always been regarded as the most luxurious of textile fibres and when complemented with an original hand-painted design, the finished fabric has a sheen and glow quite unlike anything which can be produced by machine.

It is the silkworm, a species of the caterpillar, which produces silk. The cultivated variety feeds solely on mulberry leaves and at one stage of its evolution, it spins itself a cocoon of very fine, elastic threads which can be as much as 3,000 metres, or nearly 10,000 feet in length. This thread is also very strong and when it is woven into fabrics which may appear to be delicate, will stand up to normal wear and tear, although not to excessively rough handling.

Silkworms have been kept in China for over 4,000 years and, at one time, the penalty for smuggling them out of the country was death. As a result, only the finished fabrics reached the outside world, along the famous 'silk route' to Europe. In the sixth century, monks are believed to have hidden the eggs of the silkworm in their staffs and smuggled them into Byzantium. In the twelfth century, silk was produced in Italy and in France, the first silk was woven in Lyons in the sixteenth century.

Painting on silk, which was by then highly developed in the Far East, was now taken up in France and French style and techniques came to influence the rest of the Western world. Sadly, the art declined in popularity and was forgotten until early in the present century, when it was rediscovered in southern France and Brittany.

Two attributes are essential for the silk artist: not necessarily drawing skill and colour sense, as might be expected, so much as patience and diligence. With these two qualities the basic skills of painting on silk can quickly be mastered, for the craft is not as difficult to work as it may appear. Nowadays even an amateur can achieve excellent results with modern silk paints and, once the basic techniques are understood, this exciting craft can be used to produce your own uniquely original designs.

Although silk painting is not an exorbitantly expensive hobby, it is certainly not cheap for, of course, silk is a precious material, nor can it be guaranteed that your first attempt will be a masterpiece! If you are a complete beginner it is best to start with a small-scale design on a remnant of silk. Once you begin to experiment, however, you will soon discover what a wealth of possibilities there are in painting on silk, for no other technique or material can produce such luminous colours or magical results.

The opening section of this book deals with the materials required and explains the basic techniques involved. It then goes on to give a wide range of soft furnishing designs, from cushions and wall hangings to bed covers and lampshades. Each design is shown in full colour, together with details of the materials required, the methods used and a simple-to-follow chart of the painted motif. The first of these designs takes the beginner step-by-step through their first project and points out likely errors and how to remedy them.

Whether you are an experienced artist working in a studio, or a complete novice painting on a kitchen table, it is possible to learn from this book. The competent artist will draw inspiration for silk painted designs from his surroundings; the beginner, on the other hand, will find the diagrams in this book an ideal way of learning painting techniques and a means of gaining confidence.

Opposite: *two cushions, one showing a delicate rose motif, the other an orchid, against a striking blue background. Designed by Catherine d'Angeli. See page 36 for charts and instructions.*

How to begin

Once you have mastered the basic technique, this exciting craft can be used to produce luxurious and original soft furnishings at relatively low costs.

There are three different methods used for painting on silk; gutta or resist, watercolour, and salt or alcohol techniques. The gutta or resist method can be used on its own to produce very simple, stylised motifs in a single colour. The watercolour method can also be used alone for very muted, abstract designs where one colour flows into another. Most designs, however, are based on a combination of these first two methods. Salt, or alcohol, is applied to a completed painting to give a stippled effect to certain areas, but is not used as a separate method. Both agents affect the density of the paint colour; salt will darken it in mottled areas and alcohol lighten it.

Before attempting to paint on silk it is important to appreciate that you will never be able to reproduce an exact replica of any illustrated design. Silk is a natural fibre and, much like wool, varies in quality and texture. Paints may also vary in thickness and colour from one manufacturer to another. Another point to bear in mind is that a design may originally have been drawn free-hand, without any clear lines of reference, so is a 'one-off', not to be repeated. These factors, however, greatly add to the fascination of this craft, as you will always produce your own unique design.

Make sure you have everything you will require to hand before beginning any project. You will need to work quickly to achieve satisfactory results and if you have to break off in the middle of an operation because you have forgotten to buy a brush fine enough to paint small areas, the whole process could be ruined. You will also need a steady hand and eye, so make sure you are not interrupted once you have commenced a painting!

You need not make any vast initial outlay on tools or materials. Scraps of silk can be found on most remnant counters at prices to suit all purses. Keep to a few basic paint colours for your first project. Don't go to the expense of purchasing a frame for a small item; you may already possess an embroidery frame which would make a suitable alternative. Or, if you can handle a screwdriver, it is a simple matter to make a fixed frame to any size.

Basic equipment

The tools required for painting on silk are easily obtainable from art and craft shops, or by mail order from specialist suppliers. The beginner's kit should contain the following:

A wooden frame, fixed or adjustable
Tracing paper
Silk fabric
Silk paints in two or three colours
Small white mixing cups and a container for water
Gutta, or resist agent, or water-solvent resist agent
Paper cones or resist applicators
Gutta or resist colourants, or coloured resist
Thinner and fixing agents, as recommended by the manufacturer of the range of paints being used
Special salt from silk paint suppliers, or fine or coarse cooking salt
Ethyl rubbing alcohol
Two or three soft watercolour-type brushes
Pencil and white eraser fluid
Push pins or three-point thumbtacks
Ruler
Adhesive tape
Cotton wool or cotton buds
Scissors

Opposite: some of the basic equipment used in painting on silk.

Tools, materials and basic techniques

This chapter gives details of the items and basic resist and watercolour techniques needed to begin your first venture into silk painting. Any additional material, or special methods needed to complete individual projects given in this book, will be given in the instructions for the design.

Silk fabrics

Silk is obtained from the cocoon of the wild or cultivated silkworm and, when these are dried, 31g/1oz will provide sufficient thread for 7 metres/yards of a lightweight fabric 90cm/35½in wide.

The Chinese have a system of weight gauge for silk, referred to as a 'mommie', and this term is used universally in the wholesale silk trade to indicate the weight of a fabric. One mommie equals 4.3056gm/⁵⁄₃₂oz in weight to one square metre/yard of fabric; 6 mommie is considered a lightweight quality, suitable for cushions, but a heavier weight of 8 mommie is more appropriate for clothing. As a very general guide, anything under 10 mommie is considered to be a lightweight fabric; anything over is classed as a medium to heavyweight quality.

There are many different types of silk available but a lightweight silk lining material, called Habotai, is probably most widely used for silk painting. Tussah, a type of fabric produced by uncultivated silkworms, is more commonly known as 'wild silk'. Shantung is a mixture of wild and cultivated silk.

You can also obtain silk noil, twill, pongee, crepe de chine, crepe satin, taffeta, organza and crepe georgette but not all of these qualities are ideal for silk painting and many of them will impose their own very different characteristics on to a design. Heavily-textured silks, for instance, will not take the paints evenly and they also tend to encourage a 'bridge' when the gutta is applied. This will later allow the watercolours to break through the resist line and run into each other.

For the inexperienced painter lightweight silk is easier to work with because resists penetrate it more readily and paints flow better. For your first projects keep to white silk, as this background produces clear, brilliant colours when the paints are applied. An important point to remember is that white is not represented in any range of silk paint, so the white background of the fabric is used in many designs to highlight an area, or to define outlines between blocks of colours.

You may eventually wish to experiment with cream or pastel backgrounds. In this event, the chosen background colour will be the palest shade in a design and you will not be able to introduce any white. The background colour will also have an effect on the paints you use and it may be difficult to visualize the finished colouring of a design.

It is best to hand-wash silk before beginning to paint, to remove any traces of dressing or grease. Wash in hand-warm water, rinse well then roll the fabric into a towel smoothing out any creases. When it is still damp, iron with a warm iron. This procedure should also be adopted when laundering a completed article.

Frames

Silk can only be painted successfully if the fabric is evenly stretched and freely suspended. If you intend to work on items of a specific size, such as cushions, it is best to use a fixed frame. If you plan to tackle projects of different sizes, such as lampshades or wall hangings, then it will be more practical to use a frame with adjustable tension.

Before any silk is stretched on to the frame, cover the frame with adhesive tape. It can then be easily wiped clean with a damp cloth and remains of paint from previous work will not spoil a new piece of silk.

To stretch the silk over the frame, use three-point architects' thumbtacks or push pins to secure it. The three-point tacks are particularly easy to remove and will not tear the silk.

On a fixed frame, begin by pinning the four corners in place, stretching the silk and keeping it parallel to the edges of the frame. Next, secure the middle of each side, then at intervals of no more than 5cm/2in round all the edges. The silk needs to be stretched evenly over the frame and as tightly as a drum.

To fix the silk to an adjustable frame, set the frame to the approximate dimensions of the silk you are using. Pin the fabric to the movable bar and then on to the parallel fixed bar. Continue as given for a fixed frame, placing the pins approximately 5cm/2in apart while you stretch the silk. To do this, release the two screws on the movable bar and gently pull to stretch. Do not pull too hard or you may rip the fabric. When you have obtained a taut stretch, tighten the screws.

Gutta or resist

The flow of paints is controlled by a product called 'resist'—a thick, colourless liquid sold in bottles or cans. When a thin line of resist is drawn on silk, it penetrates the fibres and stops the flow of the paints. There are two types of resist readily available; gutta, which is rubber-based, and a water-soluble resist. Both types should be shaken well before use.

The most popular way to apply gutta or resist for outlining a design is with a metal-tipped applicator bottle; water-soluble resist should only be applied by this means. A cone made of tracing paper is a suitable alternative for rubber-based gutta, but the success of this method will depend on the size of hole from which the gutta will be squeezed. When using an applicator, or a cone, it should be held like a pencil but do not slant it too much.

Making a cone: cut a rectangle 14 by 18cm/5½ by 7in from a piece of tracing paper. Begin by folding the paper at a 30 degree angle towards the top, then roll the paper round the triangle. Make sure that the hole at the tip is no larger than a fine needle or pin.

To close the cone, first roll a small piece of adhesive tape around the tip, making sure it does not go over the edge and block the hole. Close the remaining openings with tape, except for the top into which the gutta will be poured.

Consistency of resists: gutta is usually ready to use. It should not be too thick, which can happen when the solvent evaporates. To dilute, add a few drops of gutta solvent. Test gutta by dipping a toothpick into the liquid and holding it over a mixing cup; if the gutta forms a thin trickle, the consistency is right. Try it out on silk. Overly thick or thin gutta will not control the flow of paints. Moreover, overly thick gutta does not dry easily and will remain sticky. Water-soluble resist is ready to use and should not be diluted.

Colouring gutta: if you wish to obtain a bright colour, put a pea-sized drop of gutta colourant into a small bowl; use about quarter of that quantity for a pastel gutta. Dilute with a thimbleful of gutta solvent and add enough gutta to fill the applicator half full. Pour the mixture into the applicator—if you are using a cone, seal it with tape.

Water-soluble resist can be discreetly coloured with only a few drops of silk paint.

Silk paints

For the projects in this book, we have used readily-available traditional silk paints. They may be diluted with a solution of 50% water and 50% ethyl rubbing alcohol, or use the special dilutant available for this purpose.

The colour chart shows pure colours which are labelled, and in the column on the right of each colour, diluted versions of the colours are shown. Colours of the same range can be mixed to create new colours or different tones and shades, for example, vermilion plus yellow equals orange. Colours from different ranges or from different manufacturers, however, should never be mixed. Also, it is not advisable to use gutta or fixatives of one make in combination with paints of another make.

Always test each colour on a sample strip of silk before using it directly on your project. Use white containers to mix your paints.

Some examples of silk paint colours

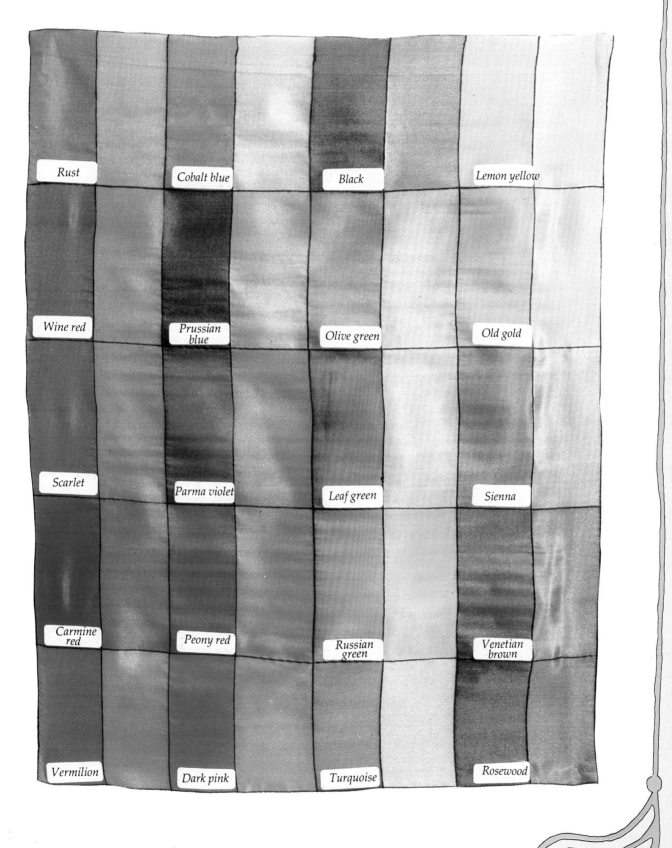

Rust

Cobalt blue

Black

Lemon yellow

Wine red

Prussian blue

Olive green

Old gold

Scarlet

Parma violet

Leaf green

Sienna

Carmine red

Peony red

Russian green

Venetian brown

Vermilion

Dark pink

Turquoise

Rosewood

Quantities of paint needed: it is important to estimate ahead how much paint you will need, particularly for large even areas and when mixing colours. The heavier the silk, the more paint it will absorb. For example, to cover the background on one square metre/yard of 6 mommie silk you will need about 40gm/2oz of paint but for the same background on twill, you will need approximately double this quantity.

Blending paints: there are two ways of accomplishing this within an area which has been treated with resist.

1) Use paints straight out of the bottle. Place the different colours you have chosen side by side, by dipping your brush directly into one of the bottles, rinsing, then dipping it into the next, and so on. Work fast, so that the surface does not dry. If you want a lighter area, leave it white. While the surface is still wet, rinse the brush again, pick a small amount of the water/alcohol solution and use that over the entire surface, rubbing it a little to allow the colours to blend.

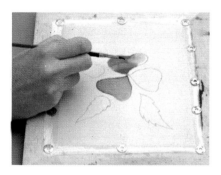

2) If you are working with a large area and you are concerned about being able to paint quickly with different colours, prepare the paints in small containers instead. In some cases only a few drops will be sufficient. Apply the paints side by side, allowing them to intermix, without rinsing the brush as you go along. Avoid using too many containers and colours, so as not to become confused or have a lot of waste.

Textile paints: these paints are creamy in consistency and are set with an iron. When used without water they do not bleed on the fabric. They can be used to highlight certain details in a design.

Anti-fusant: traditional silk paints flow into each other on a fabric which has not been treated with resist outlines. An interesting new way to paint while having a certain level of control is with an anti-fusant. You can buy this produce ready for use, or prepare it yourself by mixing 20% gutta with 80% ethyl rubbing alcohol.

Shake the liquid well, spread over the entire area where you wish to avoid bleeding with a brush especially reserved for this purpose and rinsed in alcohol, then allow to dry. A thin layer is all that is needed. Pick up a small amount of paint with a separate brush and apply over the anti-fusant. The paints will not bleed.

Use this method for fine detailed painting without resist. Use different shapes of brushes to obtain a great variety of effects.

Proceed as usual after painting with steam setting and washing. The anti-fusant will come out and the fabric will retain its free-hand painted design.

Brushes

Use a brush to apply paints to silk. Your brushes should be of good quality but not necessarily sable brushes. One fine brush and a thicker one will be sufficient for your needs. To cover large surfaces with the same colour, rather than a brush use a piece of cotton wool soaked in the required colour. Special foam brushes and foam applicators can also be used.

14

Painting backgrounds: once paints are applied to silk, they dry very quickly. To obtain an even background *never* go back over a dry area with a wet brush, or place wet paint next to dry paint if there is no resist to separate them. You would then have a dark edge line which is usually difficult, if not impossible to correct.

You must therefore work quickly and to cover large surfaces use foam brushes. Remember to have a fine brush handy for filling in any nooks and crannies you may have missed. See to it that the surface remains wet. Where there is a central design, paint alternately on both sides of this, so as to keep both sides wet.

Fixing the paints

Once the painting is completed, the colours must be 'set' so that they will not run in laundering, or fade with exposure to light—this process is referred to as 'fixing'.

Prior to fixing, the painted silk is extremely fragile and must be handled carefully. It is sensitive to water, alcohol and light. Three methods of fixing can be used but follow the paint manufacturer's instructions and remember that you must never mix different types of paint and fixatives.

1) Brush-on fixative: for some ranges of paint the manufacturers recommend a fixative in liquid form. This is brushed on after the paints are dry with a broad, stiff brush—make sure all the fabric is well covered. Leave to dry for one hour or the period of time recommended by the manufacturer.

Remove the fabric from the frame and handwash in *cold* water. During this process some surplus dye may be removed, as well as any gutta used. Hang up to dry and, finally, iron. The colours should now be permanent and set for handwashing (30°C or 86°F) and some methods of dry-cleaning.

2) Iron-setting paints: some water-based paints can be fixed by using an iron set to the temperature recommended by the manufacturer.

After the paints are dry, remove the silk from the frame, taking care that it does not touch any damp surface. Iron the silk all over the 'wrong' side. If the recommended iron temperature is too high for the fabric, protect it with a piece of plain white paper between the iron and the fabric. This method will set the colours permanently for handwashing.

3) Steam-setting paints: alcohol-based paints are best fixed by steaming. Purpose-built steam ovens are available but are rather expensive. As an alternative, it is possible to use a pressure-cooker.

After the paints have dried for some hours, remove the fabric from the frame and roll it very carefully into a larger piece of absorbent paper; white blotting paper or wall-paper liner are ideal. The silk must be absolutely flat, with no wrinkles or creases and must not overlap or touch itself. Roll the paper and silk into a sausage-shape of about 4cm/1½in diameter. Close the roll with

masking tape, or adhesive tape, and also seal the ends.

Wrap the roll loosely in aluminium foil. Partly-fold the ends of the parcel to allow steam to enter but prevent condensation running into the centre of the parcel, so damaging the painted silk. Fill the pressure cooker with 2cm/¾in of water, or not quite to the base of the perforated basket, (see Figs a and b). Fit the foil-wrapped parcel, folded ends facing downwards, into the basket without touching the sides, place the basket on the trivet inside the pressure-cooker and close. Raise the pressure to 2.3kg/5lb per square 2.5cm/1in and steam for about 45 minutes.

If a pressure-cooker is not available, use a large pot with a well-fitting lid but treble the fixing time. Do not allow the pot to boil dry!

fig a shows the inside of a pressure cooker

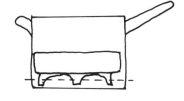

fig b shows the level of water in the bottom of the cooker

Salt and alcohol techniques

Once the painting has been completed, marvellous mottled and spotted effects can be achieved by either applying salt to certain areas while the silk is still wet, or alcohol when the silk is dry. These techniques can also be combined in one design.

With both techniques, discretion is best. Be careful not to use too much salt and scatter it well, otherwise you may get a muddled effect. Use a small brush to apply the alcohol, pick up a small amount and then blot your brush before beginning. The alcohol spreads quickly—you can always add more but you cannot take away!

Humidity plays a role in these techniques. With the salt, be sure it is completely dry for maximum effect and that the fabric is wet. With the alcohol, the fabric must be completely dry to produce a mottled effect.

Salt technique: this consists of scattering various kinds of salt over a wet surface. You can use coarse salt, table salt or salt crystals. Each grain of salt will attract the paint towards it by absorbing the water. The result is a lovely spotted effect which is completely unpredictable.

Alcohol technique: this is obtained by placing a brush dipped in alcohol on to a dry painted surface. The alcohol repulses the colour and thereby produces light coloured spots, surrounded by an outline of concentrated colour.

Above: applying salt to a wet fabric.

Below: applying alcohol to a dry fabric.

Opposite: the effects achieved with the salt technique.

How to enlarge or reduce a design

The following pages in this book give diagrams of designs and motifs which you can copy. To enable them to fit into the page size they have been considerably reduced and to produce the size indicated in the instructions, the design must be traced out to the measurements given on the squared grid. As an example, if the measurement for one square of a grid is given as 3cm/1¼in and the design covers ten squares, the finished size of the painting will be 30cm/11¾in, (see Figs a and b). For conversions from centimetres to inches, see page 4.

You may, of course, wish to enlarge the actual drawing still further, or even reduce it, and there are several ways which will enable you to obtain an exact copy. Various forms of photocopiers will enlarge or reduce a diagram on paper and more sophisticated machines will copy a design to any size, on any material, but these are rather costly.

The simplest way to enlarge or reduce a drawing, however, is to use a pantograph, which you can either make yourself, or obtain from most art or craft shops, (see Fig c). A pantograph consists of four flattened rods, or pieces of wood. At the appropriate points, a tracing point is fixed to these rods for tracing over the lines of the original, and a drawing point for making the copy. The pantograph is hinged at the crossing points and can be adjusted to enlarge or reduce the copy.

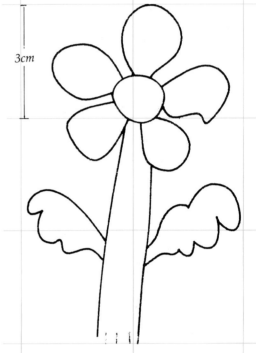

fig a

design for enlarging

fig b

3cm

enlarged design to correct measurements

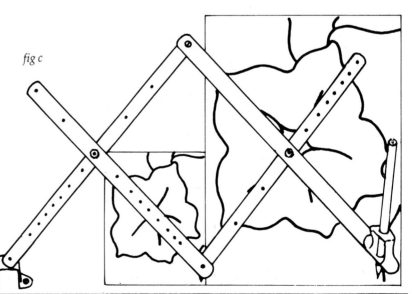

fig c

drawing of a pantograph

How to transfer designs on to silk

Once you have produced a drawing to the correct size needed for the design you have in mind, there are two ways of transferring it on to the silk.

1) Place tracing paper over the drawing and trace over the outlines with a heavy, waterproof marker. With the silk stretched tightly over the frame, place the traced design under the silk and hold it lightly in position with adhesive tape at the corners. Outline the design directly with resist, then remove the taped tracing and proceed to paint.

2) For greater precision, trace the design with a pencil on the wrong side of the tracing paper. Place the tracing paper wrong side down over the silk, which is placed flat on a table, and go over all the outlines again. The pencil lines will show lightly on the silk and when the silk is stretched over the frame, you will be able to outline the design with resist.

Your first try

Size of silk pieces: if you are a beginner, choose a small project. You will find it easier to work with and you will also avoid waste. For our first sample, we have used a rectangle 43 × 32cm/17 × 12½in.

Type of silk: choose 6 mommie white silk, see under 'silk' on page 10. You might also like to try working with a heavier silk such as twill to see how the work differs depending on the type of silk you use.

Frame: use either a fixed or an adjustable frame. We suggest that beginners make several tests with different equipment and supplies before attempting more complex projects.

How to apply the resist: hold the cone or applicator like a pencil. Always have a paper towel ready to wipe away any drops which may form at the tip of the applicator. Should these drops form too quickly, it is a sure sign that the hole is too large. Always begin painting at the upper left-hand corner of the design (or the upper right-hand corner if you are left-handed).

How to apply the paints: choose the larger brush. Start painting in the centre of an enclosed shape and allow the paints to bleed towards the resist line.

Errors and corrections

Let us go over your first sample and see what you should not have done and find out how you can correct the errors you may have made.

Resist mistakes: never leave a gap or opening (even a tiny one) in the line of resist outlining a shape.

The silk should not touch the work surface when you are applying the resist (this can happen if the silk is not taut). If the silk does touch the surface, the resist will spread and smear.

Never use overly thin or overly thick resist. That will cause the colours to bleed through.

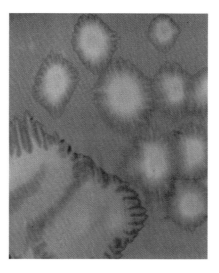

Paint mistakes: never go over an already dry surface with a wet brush.

Never allow a surface to dry if you are planning to place another colour right next to it for blending. A dark edge line will appear if you do. Never apply a large quantity of paint next to the resist outline because then the overloaded area might breach the resist line.

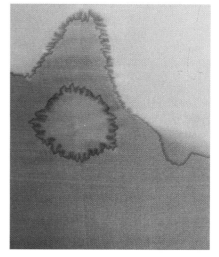

How to correct certain mistakes: spots and dark edge lines can be used to obtain decorative effects.

You can correct a badly applied background in two ways:

(a) By re-moistening it and scattering coarse salt over it (details of this technique are given on page 16).

(b) Paint lighter shapes with pure alcohol (see page 16).

These are the only techniques which can help you to correct spots caused by water, alcohol, dark edge lines or uneven colour on a larger surface.

It is possible to remove a dark edge line or spot on an already painted small surface by covering that area with pure alcohol. Use a brush to absorb any excess paint that might accumulate around the edges. Rub the line with the brush, then apply the paint once more.

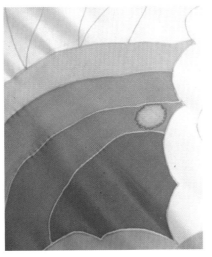

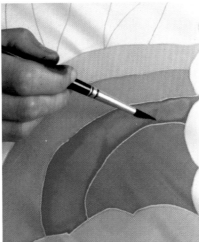

On a white surface, rub the spot with a cotton swab soaked in alcohol, being careful not to touch any nearby painted areas.

Do not be discouraged if your first project is not perfect. Start all over again, and keep telling yourself that hand-crafted items often show slight imperfections which set them apart from machine-made articles.

Silk cushions

Luxurious cushions are practical yet ornamental items of soft furnishing and need not be expensive. The beauty of your own original silk cushions will add the finishing touch to any room and highlight a colour scheme. Even if you are not an experienced needle-woman, making a cushion presents few problems. If you can cut a straight edge and sew a plain seam, you can make a successful cushion.

First determine the size of the cushion you intend to make—46cm/18in square is a popular size. For the cover you will need to buy sufficient silk for the painted front of the cushion and a similar amount of silk, or a co-ordinating material, for the plain back. As a guide, for a cushion cover with a silk front and back, a length of 51cm/20in from a 102cm/40in wide fabric will be enough to cover a 46cm/18in cushion. This will allow about 2.5cm/1in all round for seaming.

Ready-made pads to fit inside the cushion cover are available in different shapes and sizes from most furnishing departments and stores. It is not a good idea to fill the cover with loose kapok as not only will this go lumpy in use, but the cover cannot be removed for cleaning purposes.

To make a cushion cover

Place the completed silk painting, already fixed and pressed, together with the remaining piece of silk or backing material, with the right sides facing each other. If seaming the cushion by hand, tack along three sides of the square about 1cm/½in in from the edge. If machining the cushion, use a soft crayon and rule to trace a line about 1.5cm/⅝in in from the edges, then pin them together. Insert the cushion pad very gently and check that it will fit snugly; if not, re-tack or re-pin the seams. Remove the cushion pad.

Seam round the edges by hand, using small neat, back-stitches, or by machine. Turn the cover right side out and insert the cushion pad. To close the remaining seam, turn about 1cm/½in along both edges to the inside and slip-stitch them together by hand, keeping the stitches small and neat so that they barely show.

To remove the cover for cleaning, it is a simple matter to snip through the slip-stitches and re-move the pad. Once the cover has been cleaned, re-insert the pad and stitch it in position again.

Right: marking the seam allowance for a cushion cover along three edges on the wrong side of the fabric.

Right: machining round three edges of a cushion cover on the wrong side of the fabric.

Professional hint

To give a perfect fit at the corners of a square cushion, surplus fabric should be removed to ensure that there are no unsightly lumps. Before turning the cover to the right side and inserting the pad, trim each corner diagonally across, (see Fig a), taking care not to cut too closely to the stitches.

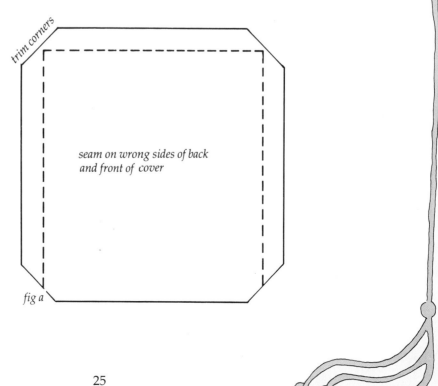

trim corners

seam on wrong sides of back and front of cover

fig a

Dahlia cushion

This cushion measures 40cm/16in square when finished.

Materials

Fabric: 46cm/18in white silk 6 mommie, 92cm/36in wide.

Paints: olive green, sienna, golden yellow, lemon yellow, rust, vermilion, rosewood, Russian green and combinations of these colours as well as diluted versions.

Gutta: beige, add a very small amount of red and black colourant to the gutta.

Method examples

For frame around background use rust diluted: for background, lemon yellow diluted.

To shade the petals, begin at the base. Begin by placing some rosewood, then rust, then orange, then yellow. Leave a small white space between each. Use a paint brush or cotton swab and blend the colours into each other. Vary the shades from one petal to the next.

Shade leaves in same way.

Professional hints

When using a ruler to obtain a straight line for framing the background, keep the tip of the cone or applicator away from the ruler.

Be sure to secure the silk on the frame as straight as possible so that the line will remain straight after the frame is removed. When painting large areas, start at the upper left-hand corner and continue painting in two directions at the same time.

To make your work easier, extend the leaves at the top of the design until they touch the edge of the silk. You will then be able to paint in one direction.

Opposite: a burst of vivid colour to brighten up a room. For chart, see page 28.

chart for dahlia cushion

2cm

chart for iris cushion

2cm

Iris cushion

This cushion measures 40cm/16in square when finished.

Materials

Fabric: 46cm/18in white silk 6 mommie, 92cm/36in wide.

Paints: Parma violet, Prussian and cobalt blues, Russian green, sienna, golden yellow, vermilion, carmine red, wine red, lemon yellow, rust and combinations of these colours as well as diluted versions.

Gutta: natural, slightly coloured with yellow.

Method examples

For frame around background use wine red and a very small amount of golden yellow diluted with water/alcohol: for background, very diluted sienna.

To shade the petals, see photographs on this page.

To obtain the veining effect on the petals, use one of the following techniques:

1) While the surface is still slightly damp, use a brush to pick up a small amount of Parma violet. Remove excess paint on a paper towel, then apply with light strokes.

2) When the area has dried, dip a clean brush to pure alcohol, remove excess on a paper towel and lightly stroke the areas where you wish to have a veining effect.

Professional hints

See instructions for Dahlia cushion.

Opposite: the iris, with its unique petal formation, is an exquisite flower to paint on silk. For chart, see page 29.

Bouquet cushion

This cushion measures 40cm/16in square when finished.

Materials

Fabric: 46cm/18in white silk 6 mommie, 92cm/36in wide.

Paints: peony, wine and carmine reds, vermilion, lemon yellow, sienna, Russian green, scarlet, Parma violet, dark pink, olive green, Prussian blue, black, Venetian brown, golden yellow and combinations of these colours as well as diluted versions.

Gutta: natural, coloured with very small amounts of yellow and black.

Method examples

For the background, mix sienna with the water/alcohol solution.

For the petal shading, work as described for the Dahlia and Iris cushions.

Professional hints

This is an intricate design and it will take a long time to apply the gutta. Start at the top left-hand corner.

To cover up a spot or mistake on the background, add another detail to the design. Outline this detail with gutta. Once the gutta is dry, moisten that area with alcohol and remove any paint which may have accumulated on the edge with a paint brush. When the area has lightened, paint in whatever shade you wish.

Opposite: paint a bouquet of flowers that will remain fresh for all time.

chart for bouquet cushion

2cm

Mountain village cushion

This cushion measures 40cm/16in square when finished.

5cm

Materials

Fabric: 46cm/18in Pongee 5 mommie, 92cm/36in wide.

Paints: peony red, chrome yellow, cobalt blue, cornflower blue, ultramarine, black, Prussian blue, orange and combinations of these colours as well as diluted versions.

Gutta: pale orange.

Method examples

Leave the clouds white. Above them paint a very pale graded wash blending from pale orange to cobalt blue and diluted Prussian blue. The mountain colours in the foreground are stronger than those in the background. The slopes can either be blue or blue-grey, pink or pinky-grey.

Paint the village in the same colours as the mountains with touches of chrome yellow.

Paint the stream using a variety of blues, leaving some white areas as a contrast.

For the rocks use grey, lightly blending light and darker greys with a paint brush.

Umbrella cushion

This cushion measures 46cm/18in square when finished.

Materials

Fabric: 51cm/20in Pongee 5 mommie, 92cm/36in wide.

Paints: pink, golden yellow, fuchsia, cobalt blue, Parma violet, Prussian blue, jade green, light brown, black and combinations of these colours, as well as diluted versions.

Gutta: pink, gold.

Method examples

This is a simple design. All the colours we have used have been diluted. The background stripes must be paler than the figures and umbrellas. For flesh tints add water and alcohol to a mixture of light brown and pink.

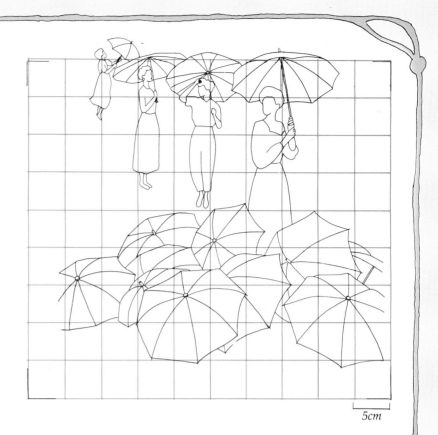

5cm

Rose and orchid cushions

These cushions measure 46cm/18in square when finished.

Materials

Fabric: 48cm/19in by 94cm/37in of white Pongee 9 mommie for each cushion (front and back are on one piece).

Paints: wine red, pink, black, olive green, jade green, dark green, chrome yellow, Prussian blue and combinations of these colours as well as diluted versions.

Gutta: natural for the flower shapes; silver for the foliage, stamens and dew drops.

Method examples

Rose cushion: the roses should be very pale. Dampen them with water, then shade the petals with touches of diluted wine red, pink, grey (black + Prussian blue + alcohol) and chrome yellow.

Use all the greens on the leaves. To make them stand out, paint a thin black line inside the gutta outline, then a dark green one; pick out the centres in pale green, with a few bright spots in diluted olive green.

Paint the background very evenly with undiluted Prussian blue.

Orchid cushion: shade the flowers carefully with mixes of very diluted wine red and pink, making the centres darker. When the flowers are dry, speckle them with a neat wine red or pink antifusant.

The leaves are painted in shades of green. To get a silvery effect, place a litle spot of grey on each leaf and with the brush dipped in water and alcohol blend it out to the edges.

Paint the background very evenly with undiluted Prussian blue.

3.5cm

chart for rose and orchid cushions

Random-patterned cushion

This cushion measures 40cm/16in square when finished.

Materials
Fabric: 46cm/18in white silk 6 mommie, 92cm/36in wide.

Paints: rosewood, lemon yellow, golden yellow, vermilion, rust and combinations of these colours as well as diluted versions.

Method examples
This example does not have any gutta lines and the paints are allowed to flow into each other.

Apply the paints in whatever manner pleases you. From time to time, place some water/alcohol solution directly on to the silk. Blend by rubbing, so that the shades mix. Apply the salt as you go along.

When everything has dried, remove the salt. Make a few spots with alcohol if you wish.

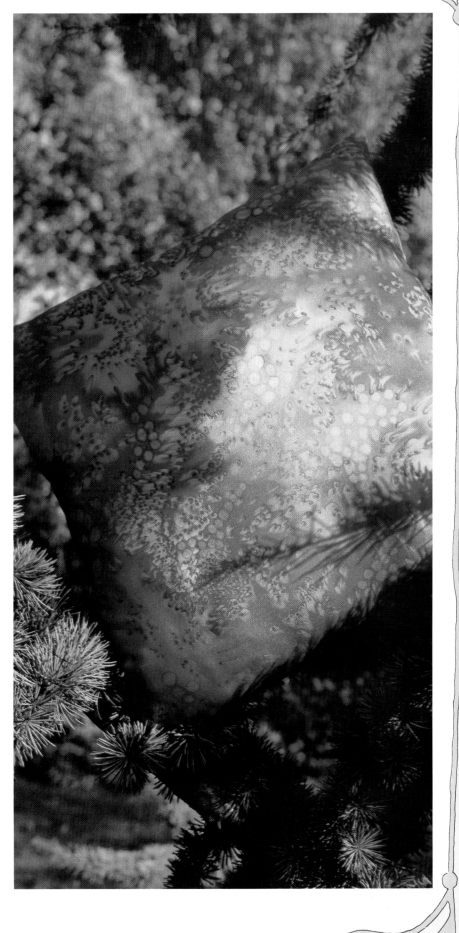

Deer by a stream

This cushion measures 40cm/16in square when finished.

Materials

Fabric: 46cm/18in white silk 6 mommie, 92cm/36in wide.

Paints: cherry, wine red, purple, golden yellow, old gold, azure, ultramarine blue, marine, black, emerald green, madeira and rosewood brown and combinations of these colours as well as diluted versions.

Gutta: grey, green and pink.

Method examples

Use each coloured gutta to match the colour in the area it will enclose.

Paint foreground leaves with pink, wine red tinted with madeira and yellow, diluted as required in some areas.

Paint tree leaves with green occasionally tinted with yellow, madeira or blue. Some leaves towards the centre of the clusters are in shades of pink, orange and madeira.

Background around deer is created with spots of pink, ultramarine, green and azure (extremely diluted). Sprinkle a few crystals of coarse salt.

For stream use greys tinted with green, blue or pink. Make a few discreet alcohol spots on dry surface.

For body of deer use gold and madeira brown. Use lighter shading in some areas to create relief. Use black for hooves. Make a few spots on body with madeira and rosewood brown while painted surface is still wet.

Opposite: capture this endearing scene of unspoilt nature.

chart for deer cushion

5cm

Lilies and wisteria cushion

This cushion measures 40cm/16in square when finished.

Materials

Fabric: 46cm/18in white silk 6 mommie, 92cm/36in wide.

Paints: azure, marine, purple, golden yellow, rosewood brown, emerald green, leaf green, Parma violet, ultramarine blue, madeira and combinations of these colours as well as diluted versions.

Gutta: natural and green.

Method examples

Use natural gutta for flowers, green gutta for leaves.

Keep lilies very light, creating relief with highly diluted madeira and golden yellow. Paint wisteria using blue and Parma violet diluted to varying shades. Paint leaves in green, occasionally lightened with a touch of yellow.

For background, make spots using blue or green hues. When surface is dry, make a few spots with alcohol.

chart for lily and wisteria cushion

5cm

Above: *creamy lily trumpets and*
gently trailing wisteria blossom are shown
on this delicate cushion.

Silk wall hangings

Painting on silk is the ideal way of creating an original masterpiece, as it allows you to combine your own unique patterns and colours.

Choose a subject for your wall hanging which will add to the atmosphere of the room; strong and bold for a living area, soft and subtle for a bedroom. Use colours which will complement the decor of the room and choose a position for the wall hanging which will allow it to be a focal point in the room without being subjected to too much direct sunlight, as this will gradually fade the colours.

To complete a wall hanging

In addition to the completed silk painting, already fixed and pressed as directed by the manufacturer of the paint, you will require a piece of white cotton batiste the same size as the wall hanging. You will also need four semi-circular lengths of wooden dowelling, 2.5cm/1in in diameter, to the width of the hanging and allowing 2cm/¾in extra at each end, plus a tube of non-staining glue and cord for hanging the picture.

Place the silk painting together with the white backing material, with the right sides facing each other. Tack, or pin along the two side edges, leaving the top and bottom open, then seam along the side edges. Turn to the right side and press.

Glue the first length of dowelling to the wrong side of the lower edge of the hanging, as illustrated, then glue the raw edges of both pieces of fabric to the dowelling. Carefully place the second piece of wood on top of the first piece, concealing the raw edges, and glue in place.

Finish the top edge of the painting in the same way, placing the length of cord between the two pieces of wood before glueing.

Professional hint

If you wish to paint or stain the wooden dowelling in a colour that will harmonise with your design, this must be done before sticking it in place.

charts for cat, bouquet and woodland wall hangings

2cm

Small wall hangings

Cat and woodland wall hangings: these measure 16cm/6½in wide and 19cm/7½in deep when finished.

Bouquet wall hanging: this measures 13cm/5in wide and 18cm/7in deep when finished.

Materials

Fabric: approximately 20cm/8in wide by 25cm/10in deep white Pongee 5 mommie.

Paints: peony red, cobalt blue, old gold, olive green, jade green, dark brown for bouquet.

Pink, dark pink, Parma violet, jade green, black for woodland.

Pink, chrome yellow, dark pink, cobalt blue, Prussian blue, jade green for cat.

Combinations of all these colours as well as diluted versions.

Gutta: Pale yellow for the bouquet; natural for the trees; pink for the window and black for the cat.

Method example

These charming wall hangings are all primitive in design and present no problems in execution.

Opposite: these small wall hangings are simple in design and execution.

Walled city

This wall hanging measures 30cm/ 11¾in wide by 39cm/15¼in long when finished.

Materials

Fabric: white silk 6 mommie, 33cm/13in wide by 42cm/16½in long.

Paints: Prussian blue, cobalt blue, black, wine red, dark pink, vermilion, sienna, old gold, Venetian brown, Parma violet and combinations of these colours as well as diluted versions.

Gutta: natural, coloured with very small amounts of red and black to obtain a light beige shade.

Method examples

For the sky dilute Prussian blue with water/alcohol solution: for the lower edge of the background, use sienna and old gold diluted.

Professional hints

Once the silk is removed from the frame, the line should be as straight as possible because of the geometric shapes of this design, so be very careful to pin the silk parallel to the edges of the frame.

The various areas should be painted evenly.

Opposite: paint a scene from the land of make-believe.

chart for walled city wall hanging

2cm

Wild duck

This wall hanging measures 30cm/11¾in wide by 43cm/17in long when finished.

Materials

Fabric: white silk 6 mommie, 33cm/13in wide by 46cm/18in long.

Paints: Prussian blue, black, cobalt blue, Russian green, olive green, sienna, lemon yellow, Venetian brown, vermilion, turquoise, rosewood brown and combinations of these colours as well as diluted versions.

Gutta: natural, coloured with small amounts of red and black to obtain light beige: coloured with white to outline the wings and feathers.

Method examples

Refer to the instructions for veining the Iris petals, see page 30, to add details to the duck.

It is recommended that you wait until the background is completely dry before proceeding with this step.

Opposite: *a bird on the wing—the ideal decorative touch for a man's study.*

chart for wild duck wall hanging

2cm

Sunset

This wall hanging measures 40cm/ 15¾in wide by 53cm/20¾in long when finished.

Materials

Fabric: white silk 6 mommie, 43cm/17in wide by 56cm/22in long.

Paints: Prussian blue, lemon yellow, golden yellow, vermilion, rust, Venetian brown, rosewood, sienna, black (to obtain bluish grey) and combinations of these colours as well as diluted versions.

Gutta: you may wish to colour slightly with yellow.

Method examples

It will take a long time to apply the gutta in this design because of the great amount of detail.

Opposite: shimmering pools and tropical plants catch the rich glow of sunset.

To make the spotted areas shown on the left, paint small spots of diluted sienna, leaving white spaces in between. Allow to dry and then add more detail, this time using pure alcohol.

chart for sunset wall hanging

2.5cm

Children flying kite

This wall hanging measures 16cm/ 6¼in wide by 20cm/7¾in long when finished.

Materials

Fabric: white silk 6 mommie, 19cm/7½in wide by 23cm/9in long.

Paints: lemon yellow, golden yellow, orange, azure, marine blue, leaf green.

Gutta: natural.

Method examples

This is a simple design and does not present any problems.

Make a few spots using vivid green across the lawn.

Gradation of trees is from vivid green to white.

Professional hint

If you wish to paint or stain the wooden dowelling in a colour that will harmonise with your design, this must be done before sticking it in place.

1.25cm

Silk lampshades

A silk lampshade can be a decorative addition to any room and is quite simple to make. The soft colours of the painted silk will add a glow to a dark corner of a room, making this medium particularly attractive for nursery lighting.

The painted silk must be mounted on to a lampshade frame and a variety of white, plastic-coated shapes are available in most handicraft stores or departments. You can also find interesting old frames in junk shops, or at local jumble sales. If these are made from bare copper wire, however, they must first be thoroughly cleaned and then painted with white lacquer and allowed to dry thoroughly, to avoid staining the silk.

The silk fabric can be mounted on to a specially prepared lampshade backing material and this method does not require any sewing. The backing is a stiffened card that can be cut to size and shape before peeling off the sheet protecting an adhesive side. The silk is then stuck down on to the adhesive, with the right side of the painting uppermost. This type of lampshade only requires a frame in two separate sections; one to hold the top rigid and one to hold the lower edge.

Mounting a lampshade: in addition to a lampshade frame you will need adhesive lampshade backing material, 3cm/1¼in less in width than the silk; double-sided adhesive tape, 2cm/¾in wide; glue, scissors, nail file and a cardboard roll.

Begin by stretching the completed silk over the adhesive lampshade backing so that it overlaps at the top and bottom by about 1.5cm/⅝in. To make this stage easier, roll the fabric on to the cardboard roll then unroll it slowly

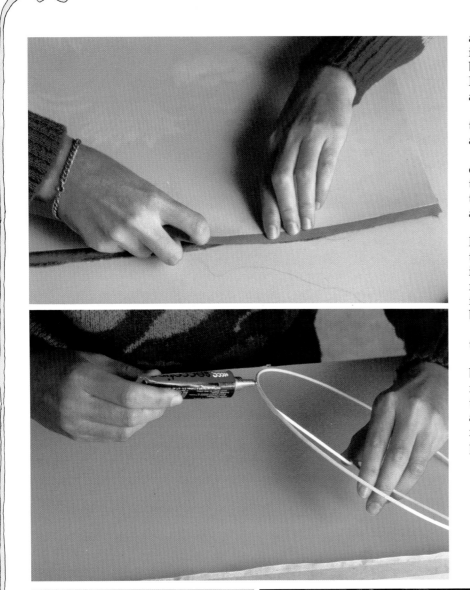

across the adhesive backing, making sure you do not create any air bubbles or creases in the process. If they do form, smooth them out as you go.

Place double-sided adhesive tape on to the overlapping parts and trim away any excess silk.

Lightly spread the glue over the outside edges of the metal rims of the frame, also over 0.5cm/⅛in of the top and bottom edges of the adhesive lampshade backing.

Roll the backing round the lampshade frame, and glue sections together. If your lampshade is oval or rectangular, make a mark at the top and bottom of the frame so that the two sides of the backing stay parallel.

Attach double-sided adhesive tape to the join in the fabric.

Cut the fabric at the top and bottom edges 1cm/½in from the metal frame. Remove the protective strip from the adhesive tape and slide the fabric under the metal frame, using a nail file or pair of scissors.

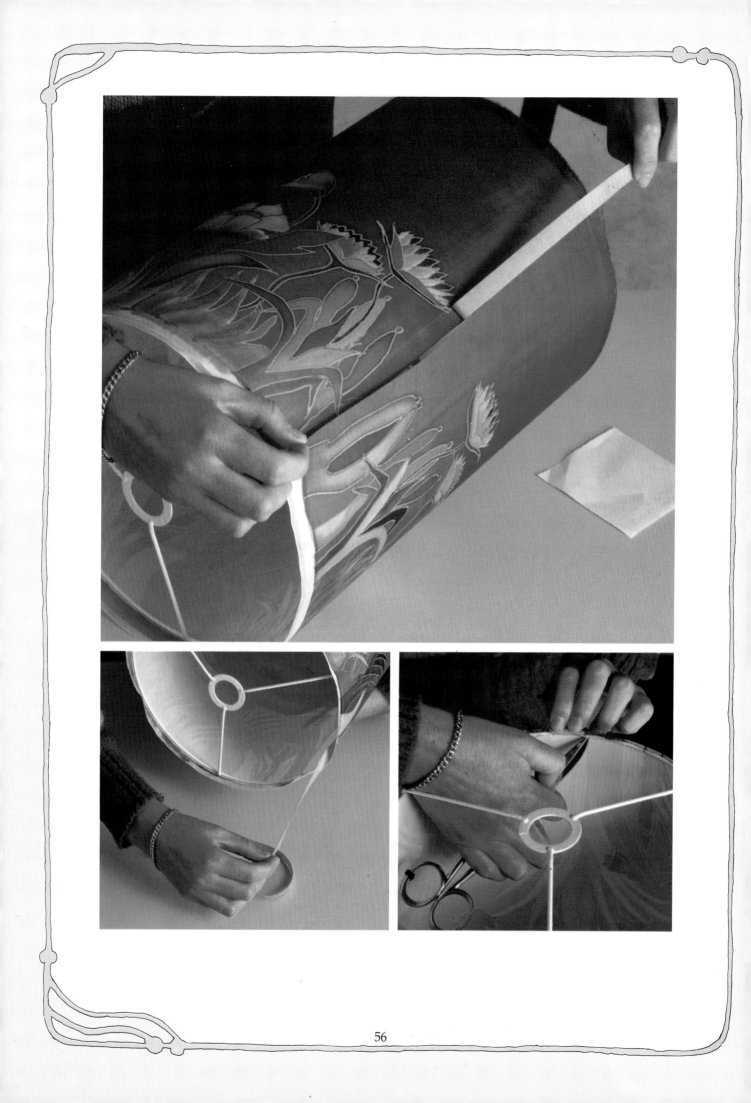

Taping a frame

Fabric which has not been mounted on card in this way needs a strutted frame, where the top and bottom rings are held in place by side struts. This type of frame must first be bound with tape, to allow the silk to be lightly stretched to the tape and stitched into shape.

Measure all the struts and the circumference of the rings of the frame and allow about two and a half times this total length in 1cm/½in wide soft, straight tape.

Bind the struts first, folding about 2.5cm/1in of the tape over the top ring and down on to the strut, (see Fig a). Wind the tape diagonally round the strut and cover the starting end. Continue down the strut, pulling the tape very taut. At the other end, take the tape behind the bound strut, over the ring and then under itself again to form a knot, (see Fig b).

Bind all the struts except one in this way.

Bind the top ring, beginning at the top of the unbound strut. Work all the way round, binding in a figure of eight where the struts join the ring, (see Fig c). Work down the remaining strut, then round the bottom ring. To finish off, turn 6mm/¼in under at the end of the tape and stitch neatly to the wrapped tape on the inside of the ring.

fig a

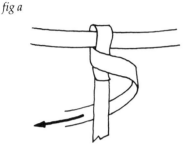

starting to bind a strut

fig b

finishing off a strut

fig c

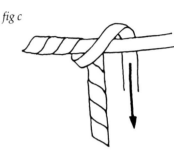

binding a top ring

Ferns

This lampshade measures 90cm/35½in circumference by 46cm/18in high when finished.

Materials

Fabric: white silk 6 mommie, 99cm/39in wide by 48cm/19in long.

Paints: leaf green, Russian green, Venetian brown, sienna, old gold, rust, vermilion and combinations of these colours as well as diluted versions.

Gutta: colour resist slightly if you wish with small amounts of black and green.

Method examples

For the background, add small amount of sienna to diluted vermilion.

Professional hints

Use a ball of cotton or a 5cm/2in foam brush to paint the background and a large paint brush when approaching the gutta areas. Always allow the paints to bleed towards resist lines.

Watch out for sections where ferns overlap. Follow each fern to keep the colours correct as you work.

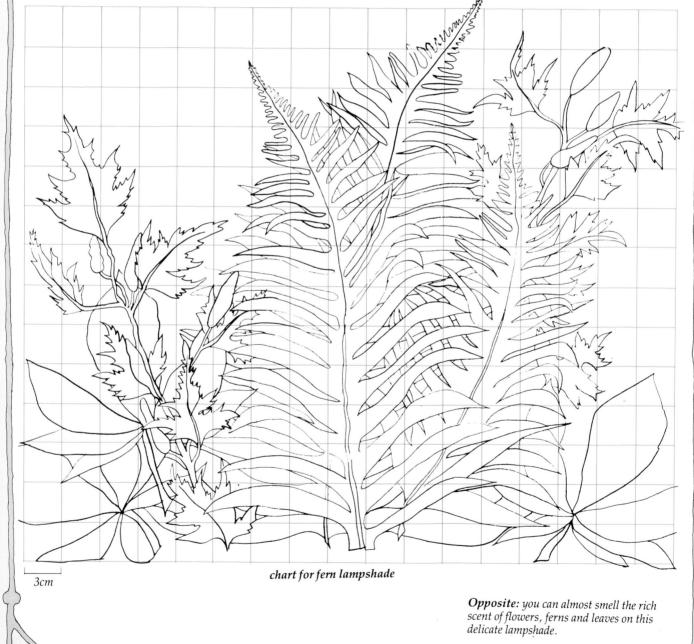

3cm

chart for fern lampshade

Opposite: *you can almost smell the rich scent of flowers, ferns and leaves on this delicate lampshade.*

Thistle wall shade

This wall shade measures 12cm/4¾in from wall edge, 25cm/9¾in wide and 23cm/9in deep when finished.

Materials

Fabric: 100cm/39in wide by 29cm/11½in deep white Pongee 9 mommie.

Paints: peacock blue, turquoise, olive green, golden yellow, chrome yellow, light brown, wine red, white fabric paint for web and combinations of these colours as well as diluted versions.

Gutta: natural for the flowers, black for the spider, green for the foliage.

Method examples

Draw the spider with black gutta. Paint the background evenly with golden yellow, diluted in the area behind the spider and web. Add touches of diluted peacock blue and turquoise.

Paint blossoms and leaves in usual way.

Allow to dry. Apply small dots of natural gutta tinted with white fabric paint and apply at random to achieve a representation of the spider's web.

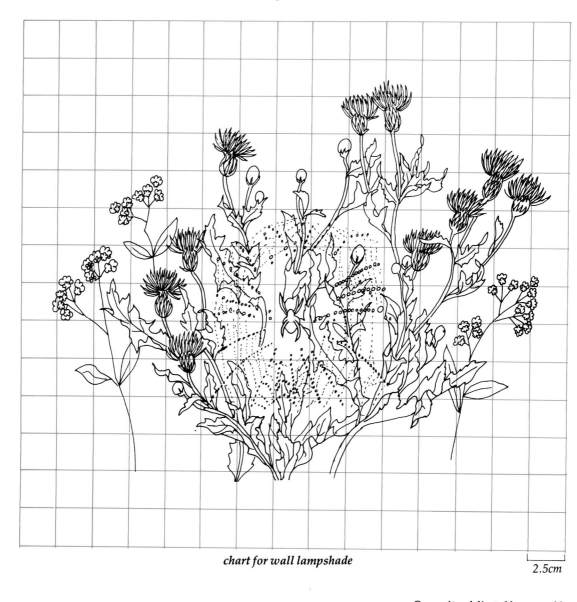

chart for wall lampshade

2.5cm

Opposite: *delicate blooms and leaves are captured on this unusual wall lampshade fitting.*

Coolie and wall lampshades

When finished the coolie lampshade measures 63cm/25in circumference around the lower edge; the wall lampshades measure 23cm/9in wide by 15cm/6in deep.

Materials

Fabric: approximately 20cm/8in deep by 69cm/27in wide white Pongee 5 mommie for coolie lampshade: 28cm/11in wide by 20cm/8in deep white Pongee 5 mommie for wall lampshades.

Paints: coolie lampshade, peony red, rust, chrome yellow, orange, old gold, jade green, olive green, light brown: **anemone wall lampshade**, pink, peony red, dark pink, old gold, orange, cobalt blue, Parma violet, black, jade green: **crown imperial wall lampshade**, peony red, orange, rust, jade green, olive green, chrome yellow, also combinations of all these colours, as well as diluted versions.

Gutta: coolie lampshade, yellow, pink, pale green: **anemone wall lampshade**, pink, blue, green: **crown imperial wall lampshade**, pale green.

Method examples

Coolie lampshade: match the gutta colours to the section outlines. Shade the red dahlias with dilutions of rust and peony red with touches of old gold and orange.

Use chrome yellow with touches of light brown for the yellow dahlia.

Blend the foliage with greens and touches of light brown, and diluted orange and old gold.

For the background use water and alcohol tinted with a little peony red.

Anemone wall lampshade: match the gutta colours to the section outlines. Shade the red anemones' petals with black mixed with orange, dark pink, peony red.

Use cobalt blue and Parma violet, with a few spots of pink for the blue anemones.

Blend the foliage with greens, more diluted in some areas than in others, and darkened in places with black or lightened in others with old gold.

For the background use water and alcohol tinted with a little orange.

Crown imperial wall lampshade: shade the blossoms in peony red and rust blended with a touch of orange.

Blend the foliage with greens, more diluted in some areas than others, with touches of diluted chrome yellow and orange.

For the background use water and alcohol tinted with a little peony red and chrome yellow.

2.5cm

charts for coolie and wall lampshades

Opposite: a riot of blossoms are used to decorate a coolie-shaped table lampshade and a pair of wall lampshades.

Iris lampshade and cushion

The cushion measures 45cm/18in square when finished; the lampshade measures 38cm/15in high by 68cm/27in circumference.

Materials

Fabric: 50cm/20in Tussah for cushion: 42cm/16½in by 72cm/28½in for lampshade.

Paints: olive green, dark brown, chrome yellow, cobalt blue, peony red, bright pink, ultramarine, wine red, old gold for the background, also combinations of all these colours, as well as diluted versions.

Gutta: gold.

Method examples

Outline the cushion and lampshade with gold gutta as usual.

Cut out tracing paper to the outline of the irises on the cushion and lampshade, also cut a 9cm/3½in radius circle from mounting board for the sun.

Fasten them to the silk with double-sided tape or a few loose stitches. Now spray the background with fabric paint or slightly diluted gold gutta.

Remove the tracing paper and mounting board. Paint flowers and leaves.

Opposite: once again, delicate iris blooms are used to decorate a cushion and matching elegant lampshade.

chart for iris lampshade and cushion

3cm

Poppy lampshade and matching cushion

When finished the cushion measures 46cm/18in square; the lampshade 24cm/9½in high by 64cm/25in circumference.

Materials

Fabric: 50cm/20in white Pongee 5 mommie for one side of cushion: 28cm/11in by 66cm/26in for lampshade.

Paints: rust, dark brown, peony red, vermilion, chrome yellow, olive green, black, Prussian blue, and combinations of all these colours, as well as diluted versions.

Gutta: red and gold.

Method examples

Put a few touches of yellow diluted with fixative on the flowers. Leave this to dry, then paint it in a graduated red to orange-yellow wash. Once the petals have dried, pick out veins with a brush dipped in alcohol.

For the seed-pods, use a mixture of greens, darkened in places with touches of black, or lightened with touches of yellow, adding dots of orange here and there.

Opposite: poppy blooms and seed heads run riot on this cushion and matching lampshade.

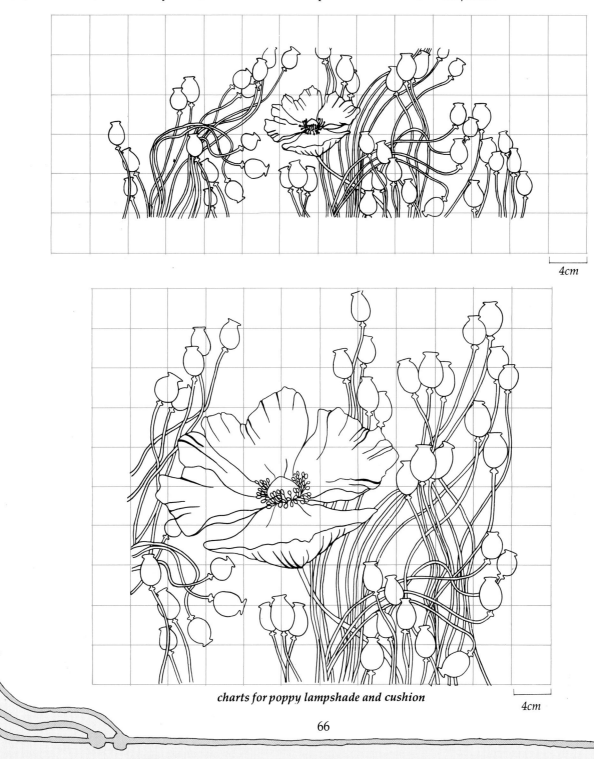

4cm

charts for poppy lampshade and cushion

4cm

Crocus and Narcissi lampshade

The lampshade measures 13cm/ 5in high by 41cm/16in circumference.

Materials

Fabric: 18cm/7in by 46cm/18in of silk crepe.

Paints: pink, fuchsia, cobalt blue, chrome yellow, peony red, jade green, olive green, and combinations of all these colours, as well as diluted versions.

Gutta: lemon yellow, cobalt blue, pale green.

Method examples

Match the gutta colour to that of the section outlines.

Shade the crocuses in blues and pinks, some parts undiluted and others diluted; use yellow in the same way for the narcissi, with a few light touches of red.

On the leaves use the greens, more diluted in some parts than in others, mixed with blue in some places and yellow in others.

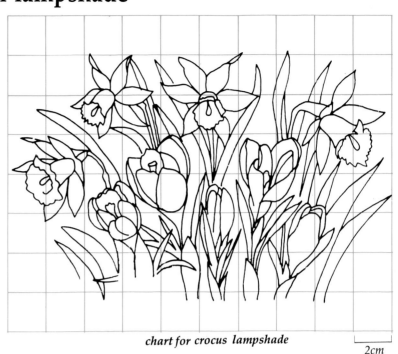

chart for crocus lampshade

2cm

Iris lampshade

This lampshade measures 18cm/ 7in high by 48cm/19in circumference when finished.

Materials

Fabric: 23cm/9in by 54cm/21½in of silk crepe.

Paints: pink, fuchsia, cobalt blue, old gold, chrome yellow, jade green, olive green, and combinations of all these colours, as well as diluted versions.

Gutta: cobalt blue, pink, pale green.

Method examples

Match the gutta colour to that of the section outlines.

Shade the flower colours with the brightest parts round the edges, lightening the colour towards the centres.

On the leaves use jade green, some parts more diluted than others, olive green diluted and mixed with yellow.

For the background use water and alcohol or special thinning liquid mixed with a little chrome yellow.

Opposite: a pair of lampshades, one featuring a variation of an iris motif, the other a design of daffodils and crocuses.

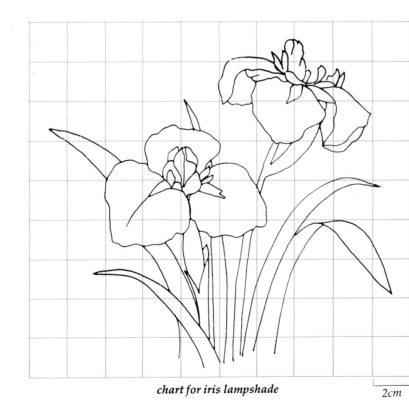

chart for iris lampshade

2cm

Bouquet lampshade and matching cushion

When finished the cushion measures 42cm/16½in square: the upper rectangle of the pagoda lampshade measures 27cm/10½in by 18.5cm/7¼in, the lower rectangle 40cm/15¾in by 27cm/10½in.

Materials

Fabric: 46cm/18in white Pongee 5 mommie for one side of the cushion; approximately 1.1m/43in for the lampshade.

Paints: peony red, wine red, chrome yellow, lemon yellow, old gold, orange, black, jade green, olive green, light brown, dark brown and combinations of these colours as well as diluted versions.

Gutta: pink, green, yellow.

Method examples

For the lampshade, make a template to fit your frame, (see diagram on page 71), placing it over the drawing of the flowers used for the cushion. Diagrams for the side panels are shown separately.

Make the cushion in the usual way, centralising the main motif.

Match the gutta colour to that of the section outlines. Shade the flowers and leaves, making veins on the leaves with alcohol once the paint has dried.

Place spots of alcohol on the bunched flower heads. Spread fixative on the irises and white flowers in the foreground. Paint greyish veins on the irises and brown spots on the white flowers.

For the background use water + alcohol, or special thinning liquid, adding peony red and yellow. Fill the spaces between the blooms with touches of green, dark brown and black.

To make up the lampshade

Make a template for the two main sides of the shade by pinning backing material to the wire frame, (see photo). Mark the cutting line with a pencil on the outside of the frame.

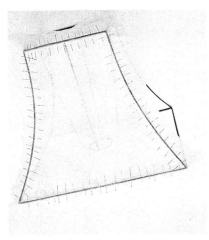

Cut out the backing material for the smaller side panels from the diagrams.

Place a strip of double-sided tape along each corner strut of the frame.

Before drawing the design, place the template for each side on the silk. Centre the design, then proceed with the gutta, paint and fixitive stages.

Place the templates on the backing material and cut out to size.

Stick the silk down on to the backing material in the usual way.

Place double-sided tape to top and bottom edges of each side.

Stick the edges of each piece to the double-sided tape on the corner struts. Hide the join on the edges with matching braid, stuck down with fabric glue.

Trim the top and bottom edges and turn under in the usual way.

charts for bouquet cushion and lampshade

5cm

Scenic lampshade and cushion

When finished this cushion measures 42cm/16½in square; the lampshade 24cm/9½in high by 80cm/31½in circumference.

Materials

Fabric: 46cm/18in white Pongee 5 mommie for the cushion; 28cm/11in by 84cm/33in for the lampshade.

Paints: pink, dark pink, cobalt blue, Prussian blue, black, lemon yellow, and combinations of all these colours, as well as diluted versions.

Gutta: pink, grey-blue.

Method examples

This design is picked out with uneven lines as opposed to straight edges. Match the gutta colour to that of the section it outlines.

Paint each area of colour from the outline downwards, lightening the colour as you go. The sky should have very pale streaks of blue, yellow and pink.

The water under the bridge is tinted with pale yellow and streaks of a stronger blue.

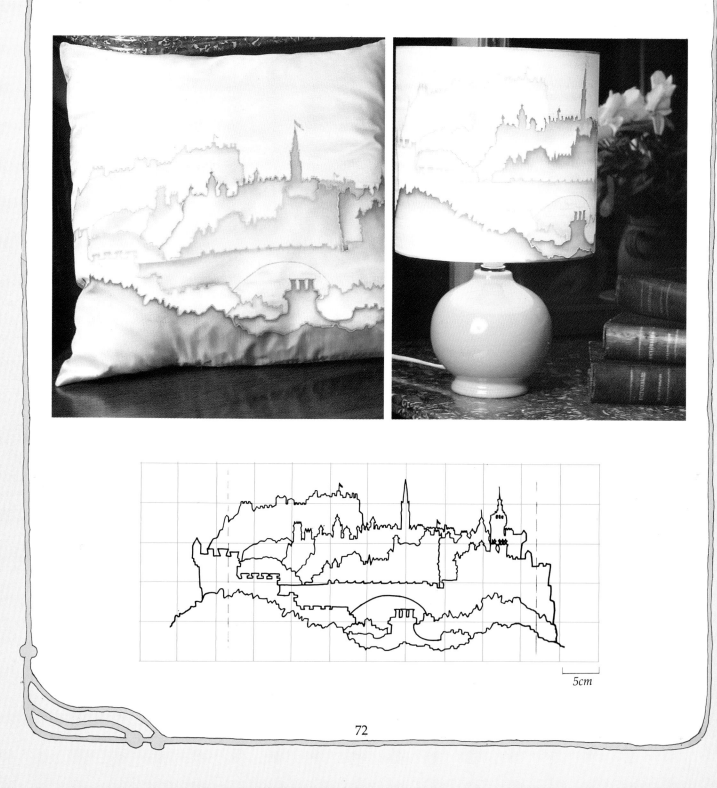

5cm

72

Cashmere lampshade

This lampshade measures 38cm/ 15in high by 95cm/37½in circumference when finished.

Materials

Fabric: 43cm/17in deep by 99cm/ 39in white Pongee 5 mommie.

Paints: peony red, pink, old gold, chrome yellow, jade green, peacock blue, black, cobalt blue, dark pink and combinations of all these colours, as well as diluted versions.

Gutta: grey.

Method examples

This design is very complicated and the gutta lines must be very fine.

Use three different greens for the design; jade, leaf green or a mixture of jade and yellow, and dark green or a mixture of jade and black.

The blue is cobalt and black, slightly diluted.

The pink is dark pink, slightly diluted.

All the other colours should be used undiluted.

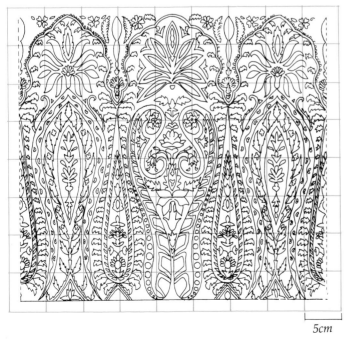

5cm

Silk tablecloths

The projects given in this book so far have all had their raw edges concealed by mounting or seaming methods. The edges of a tablecloth, however, remain visible and they must be finished off very neatly.

The design for a tablecloth should complement the decor of the room where it will be used. Pick out the predominant curtain and carpet colouring, or repeat the decorations and colouring of your china. This theme could also be repeated for a matching lampshade.

A tablecloth will require frequent laundering, so it is important to ensure that the paints are firmly fixed. Check the manufacturer's instructions regarding the method of cleaning and, if in doubt, always gently hand-wash in cool water.

To complete the edges of a tablecloth, machine hemming is possible; it is a quick method but is not really worthy of such a luxurious article. A hand-rolled hem gives the neatest result and is well worth the extra effort.

Hand-rolled hem: make sure all the edges of the silk are perfectly straight. Allow a total of 1cm/½in around all edges for the finished hem. Work a staystitch by hand, or with small machine stitches 3mm/⅛in from the raw edges. Trim the fabric away to within a few threads of the staystitch, (see Fig a).

Turn the full hem allowance to the wrong side and roll the raw edge under so that the line of staystitching just shows. Thread a fine sewing needle with the same thread and work from right to left along the hem. Sew along the hem with small, loose blind stitches—these are similar to slip-stitches—working through the staystitching and the edge of the tablecloth. Make several stitches and then gently pull up the slack in the thread, causing the edge to roll under, (see Fig b). Do not press this hem.

Machine-rolled hem: trim the edges to allow 1cm/½in hem. To hold the hem in place, turn under 6mm/¼in, and gently press along the foldline with your fingers. Turn under the remaining hem allowance to form a double hem and press with your fingers in the same way. Lightly tack in place as you go.

To complete the hem, slip it into place under the hemmer foot of the machine and stitch in place, (see Fig c). Remove tacking and press lightly.

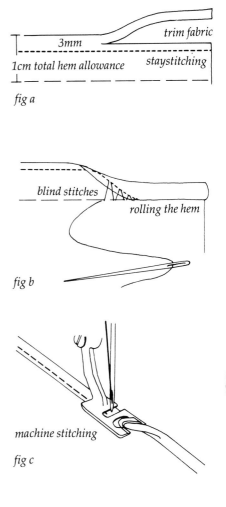

fig a

fig b

fig c

Tulip tablecloth and lampshade

When finished the tablecloth measures 90cm/36in square: the coolie lampshade measures 10cm/4in diameter at the top and 40cm/16in at the bottom.

Materials

Fabric: 100cm/39in white twill for tablecloth: 50cm/20in for lampshade.

Paints: pink, fuchsia, chrome yellow, old gold, lemon yellow, orange, cobalt blue, Prussian blue, black, jade green, light brown and combinations of these colours as well as diluted versions.

Gutta: pink and green.

Method examples

The tulips must stand out, with darker centres. Use pink tinted with black and fuchsia or light brown. Leave some areas white, next to bright or shaded parts. Some tulips should be white with grey-green, grey-yellow or grey-pink shading.

The leaves are green, or grey-green, diluted to varying degrees, tinted with cobalt blue and Prussian blue, or lightened with streaks of yellow or pink.

For the background, use water + alcohol, or a special thinning liquid tinted with a dash of black and pink.

Lampshade template

Buy a large and a small lampshade ring to your requirements, or sizes as above, plus suitable fixing mounts. Most rings are sold in diameter measurements, ie, across the widest part of the circle. Half of this measurement equals the radius; as an example, a circle with a diameter of 40cm/16in will have a radius of 20cm/8in. The circumference is measured right round the circle and to obtain this, as a *very* rough guide, multiply the diameter by three and add a further 5cm/2in. To measure this dimension accurately, multiply the diameter by 3.1416 (π *pi* or constant ratio).

To draw a template from our diagram, place a large sheet of tracing paper over graph paper; this will help you to rule straight lines. Rule a horizontal line near the bottom of the sheet and mark the centre of this as point A.

From point A rule a vertical line upwards, well extended.

Take the radius of the large circle and measure this amount to the left and right of point A, and mark as points B and C.

Decide on the height of your lampshade. Measure this from point A on the vertical line and mark as point D. The less the height of the shade, the 'flatter' the coolie shape will be.

Rule a horizontal line from point D, parallel to points B and C.

Take the radius of the small circle and measure this amount to the left and right of point D, and mark as points E and F.

Join points B—E and C—F, extending the lines to cross the vertical line and mark this as point G. This is the centre of both circles.

With a pair of compasses place the point on G and the pencil point on E, draw a circle through F: do the same for the large circle, with the pencil point on B and extending it through C. If the compass will not reach the large circle, secure a length of string to point G with a drawing pin. Ask another person to hold a pencil upright on point B and secure the pencil with the other end of the string. Hold down the drawing pin and with the string kept taut, describe the initial arc of the circle.

Beginning at point B, measure off the circumference of the large circle with a flexible tape, following the curve very carefully. Check that this measurement is the same as the circumference of the large wire ring, and mark as H.

Rule a line from H to G, noting that this will cross the curve E to F. Allow an extra amount for the overlapping join. Mark this as J. Cut out two circumferences.

Making up the lampshade

Step A: before painting the design, take a rectangular piece of silk on to which the template fits.

To transfer the template on to the silk fold it in half: fold the silk in half with the fold line either on full bias or along the thread. Mark this fold line with a pencil, then place it exactly over the fold line on the template.

Transfer the outline of the coolie shade on to the silk. Centre the design, then proceed with the gutta, paint and fixing stages, as for the tablecloth.

Place the template on backing material and cut out the shape.

Step B: spread the rectangle of silk out on a piece of blockboard and pin it taut, but not distorted.

Remove the protective covering from the backing material and stick it down on to the silk, positioned over the pencilled lines on the silk.

Unpin the silk and cut it to within 2.5cm/1in of the edges of the backing material.

Step C: begin by sticking down the extra overlap amount, after re-checking the size of the wire frame circles, H—J and B—E. Keep this edge straight.

Stick double-sided tape along the top and lower edges, turning it in at the top only.

Turn the shade upside down and push the small wire circle gently inwards, then stick the tape down over the circle.

Place the shade upright over the large wire circle and push the taped silk under this circle in the usual way.

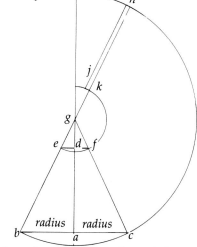

b-c-h equals circumference of large circle
e-f-k equals circumference of small circle

chart for tulip tablecloth and lampshade

5cm

Persian tablecloth and lampshade

The tablecloth measures 90cm/36in square when finished; the lampshade 31cm/12in high by 79cm/31in circumference.

Materials

Fabric: 96cm/37¾in square silk crepe for tablecloth.

Paints: pink, peony red, orange, light brown, dark brown, chrome yellow, black and combinations of all these colours, as well as diluted versions.

Gutta: beige (mix very little red, black and yellow printing ink with the gutta).

Method examples

For the tablecloth repeat the design symmetrically four times, working from the dotted lines shown on the chart.

For the lampshade carry the design outwards from the dotted lines shown on the chart, repeating once in each direction.

On the tablecloth and lampshade most of the colours on the flowers should be very diluted.

On the leaves use dark brown almost neat. Shade the flowers and the leaves.

The surround and the intertwining sections of the motif are pure peony red.

Use beige for the background, either water and alcohol or special thinning liquid undiluted with a touch of light brown.

The background of the escutcheons in the centre of the motif is dark brown, slightly diluted, with a little orange added.

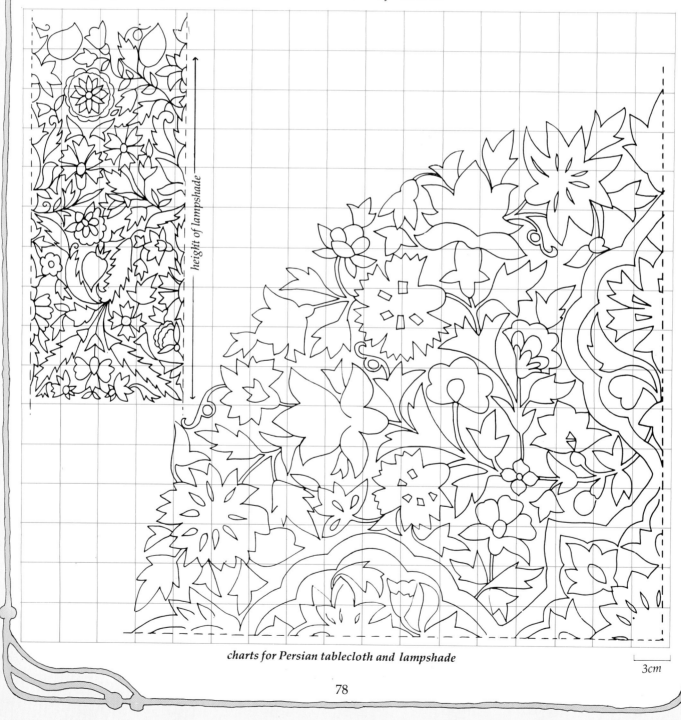

charts for Persian tablecloth and lampshade

3cm

This rich design forms a circular shape on the tablecloth and a modified version is shown on the matching lampshade.

Fruits of summer tablecloth

This tablecloth measures 90cm/36in square when finished.

Materials

Fabric: 94cm/37in square twill.

Paints: pink, peony red, chrome yellow, old gold, golden yellow, orange, turquoise, cobalt blue, marine blue, jade green, olive green, rust, light brown, black, and combinations of all these colours, as well as diluted versions.

Gutta: grey, gold.

Method examples

For the parakeet blend the colours into one another. Leave it to dry. Cover with fixative. Paint in feathers in yellow and black.

To paint the grapes drop a little water on to the centre of each grape, so creating a white spot. Using all the blues sparingly, colour each grape, taking care not to let the paint run into the white spot. Try to make them look rounded by darkening some areas with a touch of black and lightening towards the centre up to the white spot.

To paint the red flowers, shade them carefully, lightening some parts with a little yellow, darkening others with rust and light brown. Leave to dry and cover the two big flowers on the right with fixative. Paint the veins in old gold and rust (for the vein painting, work as described for the Iris cushion on page 30) and streaks in greens and yellows with dark red spots in the centres.

To paint the pink flowers use several shades of red, very diluted, with a few dashes of diluted yellow. Cover some of the flowers with fixative and then paint yellow patches and veins of rust or blue.

To paint the blue flowers use a range of blues and leave some portions virtually white. When the paint has dried, spread fixative on some of the flowers and paint in yellow veins and spots to represent the stamens.

To paint the background note that this is not worked in one colour but in several shades of grey, blue and green, diluted more in some places than others.

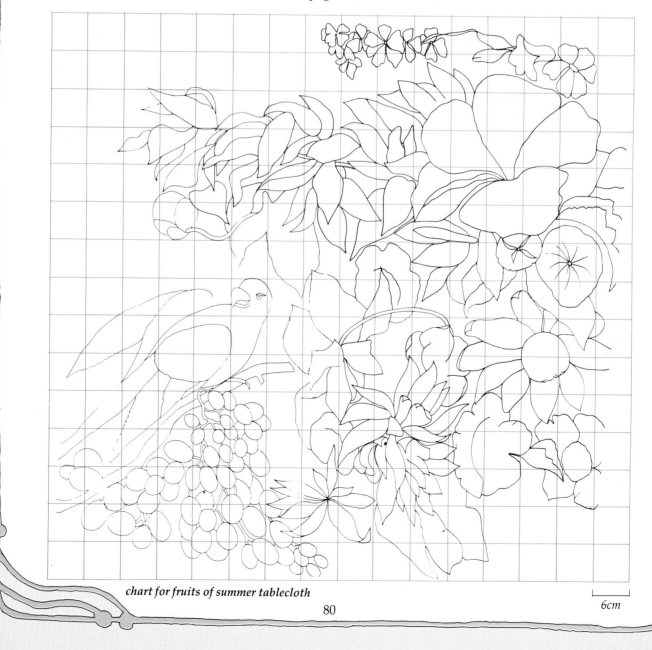

chart for fruits of summer tablecloth

6cm

*All the fruits and flowers of summer
decorate this striking tablecloth.*

Silk bed covers

The focal point of any bedroom must be the bed and its covering. It would be impractical to suggest a full-size cover made entirely from silk painted in one piece, but the addition of painted silk panels stitched to a plain background makes a feasible alternative. Another suggestion is to make the cover in separate sections, then sew them together to fit the centre of the bed and add a frill of plain silk.

The design for these panels, or sections, should enhance the decor of the room. The theme and colours could be repeated for a matching lampshade or cushions and this is a particularly effective way of decorating a nursery.

Whether you use a conventional bed cover or a duvet cover, it will require laundering, so you must ensure that the paints are firmly fixed and colour-fast. Remember, also, that the silk may need to be hand-washed and not entrusted to a machine. Where panels are required, it might be as well to provide for their simple removal by hand-stitching them in place initially. In this way they can be washed separately from the actual cover, then restitched in place. If the bed cover is made in sections, the whole item should be hand-washed.

If you are using a smooth, fairly heavy fabric for the background of the bed cover, the silk panels will show to better effect if they are lined before being stitched into position. Make sure the panels are correctly positioned, then tack them in place. Use matching thread to lightly oversew round all edges. The centre of a bed cover made in sections should also be backed with a plain lining.

chart for side panels of bedspread

82

6cm

Clematis bedspread and pillow

When finished the bedspread measures 150cm/59in wide by 200cm/78in long, plus 44cm/17in frills on three sides; the pillow measures 150cm/59in wide by 50cm/20in deep.

Materials
Fabric: 13m/14yds white Pongee 9 mommie, 92cm/36in wide, of which 4.5m/5yds will be used for the frills.
Bedspread: wadding 150cm/59in wide by 200cm/78in long; backing material 153cm/60in wide by 203cm/79in long.
Pillow: wadding 150cm/59in wide by 50cm/20in deep, 150cm/59in wide by 100cm/39in lining material, to allow for overlap.

Paints: olive green, black, red, scarlet, light brown, violet, chrome yellow, orange and combinations of these colours as well as diluted versions.

Gutta: pale grey, gold.

Method examples
Instructions for cutting out and making up are given on page 85.

On the centre panel and pillow work gold gutta around flower centres, and paint in gold streaks on red and green areas. Flowers and leaves should be carefully shaded.
Backgrounds: prepare 4litres/7pts of very diluted paint to the shade you desire, testing the colour frequently to make sure the shade is right.

Opposite: exotic birds of paradise and delicate trailing leaves and blossoms are used on the sections of this bedspread.

Painted panels: carefully paint the backgrounds very evenly around the designs.

Frills: add some vinegar to the remaining paint and pour the mixture into a large container. Dampen the frills evenly with water, then immerse into the paint mixture and stir round with your hands to ensure the paint is evenly distributed over the silk. Let them drain off a little before hanging up to dry.

Professional hint

Watch carefully while the silk is drying as the paint has a tendency to 'slip', and the silk has to be continually moved round to prevent any darker patches from forming.

chart for centre panel of bedspread

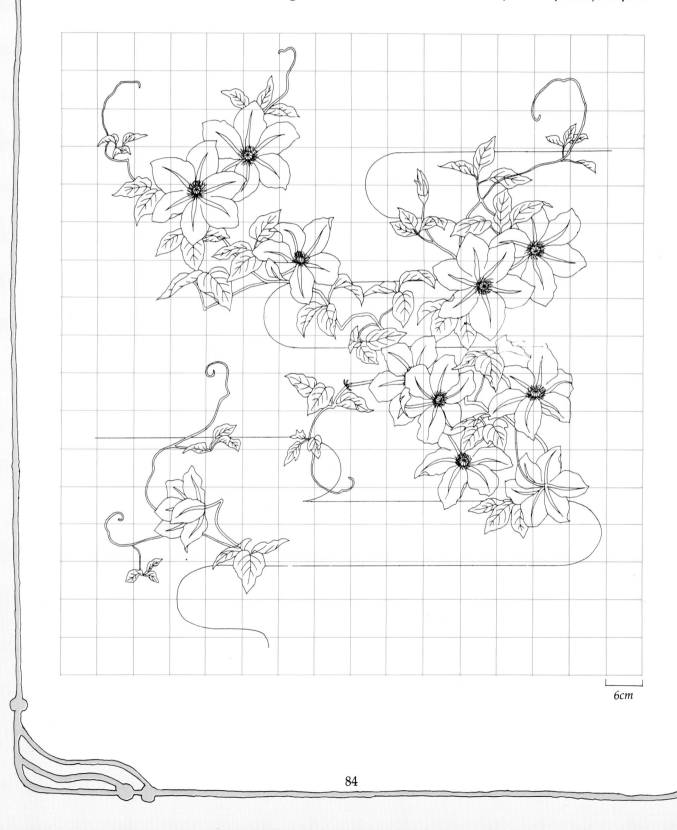

6cm

To make up

Bedspread: cut out the panel pieces to the measurements shown in the diagram on page 84, adding a 1.5cm/½in hem allowance all round. Cut out 2 lengths 45cm/18in by 4.5m/5yds for the frills.

With right sides together sew the side panels to the centre panel 1.5cm/½in in from the edges, alternating the green and red birds (see illustration on page 83). Sew the top panel to the finished piece in the same way.

Position the finished patchwork, right side up, over the wadding and tack round each panel piece to hold the material in place.

With right sides facing sew the two frills together along one 45cm/17in edge 1.5cm/½in in from the edge. Either use the selvedge as a hem for the frills, or hand-roll or machine-roll the hem (see page 74). Gather and tack the frills on to 3 sides of the patchwork 1.5cm/½in in from the edge, making sure the gathers are spread evenly round the centre piece, with the seam positioned bottom centre.

With right sides facing, machine sew the backing material, through all thicknesses, on to the centre piece, leaving the top seam open.

Turn the bedspread right side out, and slip stitch the top seam with tiny hidden stitches.

Remove the tacking stitches from the centre piece.

Pillow: Cut out the three pillow pieces as shown, then cut out two backing pieces, 37cm/14in by 153cm/60in (A) and 50cm/20in by 153cm/60in (B). Don't forget to add hem allowances all round!

Assemble the three painted pieces and wadding, following the method used for the bedspread.

Hem one long side of both A and B. With right sides facing, sew A to the lower length and sides, hem uppermost, sew B to the upper length and sides of the pillow, hem below, to overlap A.

Turn the pillow right side out and insert inner cushion.

If you do not have an inner cushion the same size as the pillow cover, make up a cushion as described on page 24, to the same measurements, and fill with feathers or kapok.

diagram for making up bedspread

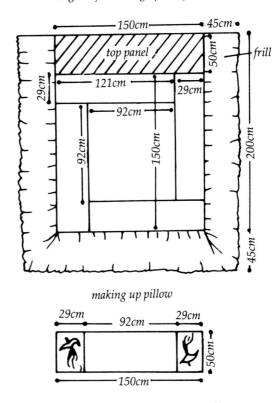

making up pillow

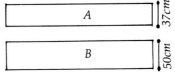

Iris bedspread

The measurements of the background material will depend on the size of the bed. The centre panel measures 94cm/37in by 135cm/53in. The corner pieces should be laid out on a 47cm/18in square.

Materials

Fabric: 100cm/39in by 138cm/55in of silk satin for centre panel and 100cm/39in square for four corner panels.

Paints: dark pink, Parma violet, pink, chrome yellow, golden yellow, old gold, rust, light brown, orange, peacock blue, jade green, olive green, dark brown, and combinations of all these colours, as well as diluted versions.

Gutta: grey-beige (to natural add a touch of black and red printing ink).

Method examples

The success of this piece depends on the delicacy of the shading.

There are three basic groups of flower colours:

Yellow irises: use different yellows, leaving some areas almost white. Darken some areas with diluted light brown and olive green. Paint in darker veins while the surface is still damp. For the vein painting, work as described for the Iris cushion on page 30.

Pink and violet irises: edge the petals with pink or violet, leaving the centres paler. The darker areas are painted in violet or pink tinged with light brown. Paint some veins in yellow while the surface is still damp.

chart for centre panel of bedspread

6cm

Rust and orange irises: edge the petals with rust, leaving the centres paler, lightly tinted with yellow or pink. Shade some areas with light or dark brown.

The leaves are worked in a variety of diluted and undiluted greens, lightened here and there with a touch of yellow and darkened with light or dark brown. A few streaks of pale pink on some of the lighter areas will add to the effect.

The border is a diluted mixture of orange and light brown.

Professional hints

Appliqué the silk panel to the centre of the backing material. Arrange the four corner pieces symmetrically, and appliqué each piece to the backing material at the same distance from the centre panel.

Opposite: the plain background fabric of this bedspread is highlighted with a central panel of multi-coloured irises and matching corner panels.

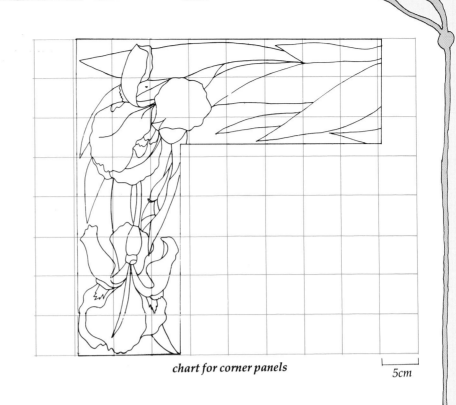

chart for corner panels

5cm

Nursery bedspread and picture

The measurements of the background material will depend on the size of the bed. When finished the centre panel measures 100cm/39in long by 77cm/30in wide, and the picture measures 44cm/17in long by 36cm/14in wide, (see page 91).

Materials

Fabric: for the background material beige cotton piqué to fit the size of the bed: for the central panel and corner pieces 152cm/60in whife Pongee 5 mommie, 92cm/36in wide: for the picture 48cm/19in by 41cm/16in white Pongee 5 mommie.

Paints: pink, orange, golden yellow, peacock blue, cobalt blue, turquoise, jade green, dark brown, light brown, black and combinations of these colours as well as diluted versions.

Gutta: black, pale beige (to natural add a touch of red and black printing ink).

Method examples

Little girl: her dress is pale pink shaded with grey. Fine salt is sprinkled on to the top of the dress to create a contrast with the smoothly painted background.

Her legs are white, shaded with grey and diluted peacock blue and her face is very light pink gently shaded with grey-blue. For her hair use old gold blended with light brown.

Little boy: his top is white shaded with very diluted light brown and a mixture of grey and diluted peacock blue. Paint his socks with diluted peacock blue shaded with grey. For his hair, blend touches of old gold, golden yellow and light brown, leaving some areas white. Use pale pink shaded with light brown and a mixture of diluted grey and peacock blue to colour his face and other skin areas.

The animals: use dark and light brown, and orange, carefully shaded from dark to almost white in some areas. While the surface is still slightly damp, use slightly diluted dark brown to paint stripes on the cat and patches on the dog.

Flowers: these are painted in diluted colours carefully graded in tones of pink, yellow, orange and turquoise.
Background: paint this very evenly with diluted pink blending into diluted orange.

Opposite: use these delightful cut-out motifs to decorate the bedspread on a child's bed and repeat the theme for a framed silk painting.

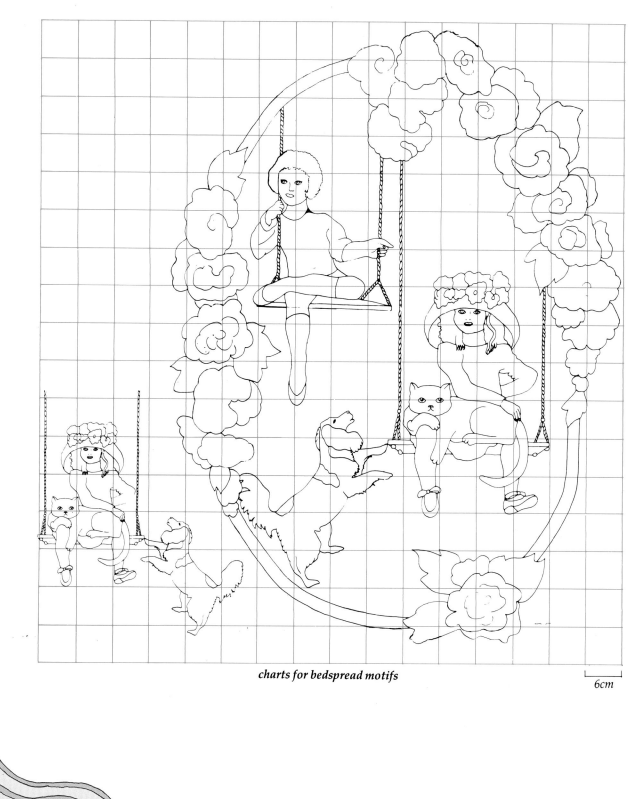

charts for bedspread motifs

6cm

Nursery duvet and lamp

This duvet measures approximately 53cm/20¾in wide by 71cm/28in long: the shade measures 76cm/30in circumference by 27cm/10½in high.

Materials

Fabric for duvet: white silk twill approximately 58cm/22¾in wide by 76cm/30in long, same amount of lining fabric and polyester wadding.

Fabric for lamp: white silk twill 81cm/32in wide by 30cm/11¾in long.

Paints: poppy red, orange, golden yellow, azure, leaf green, black, old gold, and combinations of these colours as well as diluted versions.

Gutta: natural.

Method example

This is a simple design and should not present any problems. In most cases the colours are used diluted.

To make up

Duvet: machine silk and lining together with right sides facing, leave top edge open. Turn to right side and press. Close opening with small stitches. Use fine dressmaking pins and fasten silk to lining over entire surface. Stitch silk to lining along gutta lines, matching thread to colour of gutta outlining each square. Remove pins.

In the centre of the lining of each square, make an incision about 3cm/1¼in long. Cut wadding to fit squares. Slip wadding through incision into squares. Close openings with small stitches.

Lamp: make shade as explained on page 54. Paint a motif on base of lamp if required, using matt wood paints.

Opposite: sweet dreams are ensured when baby snuggles under this dainty duvet.

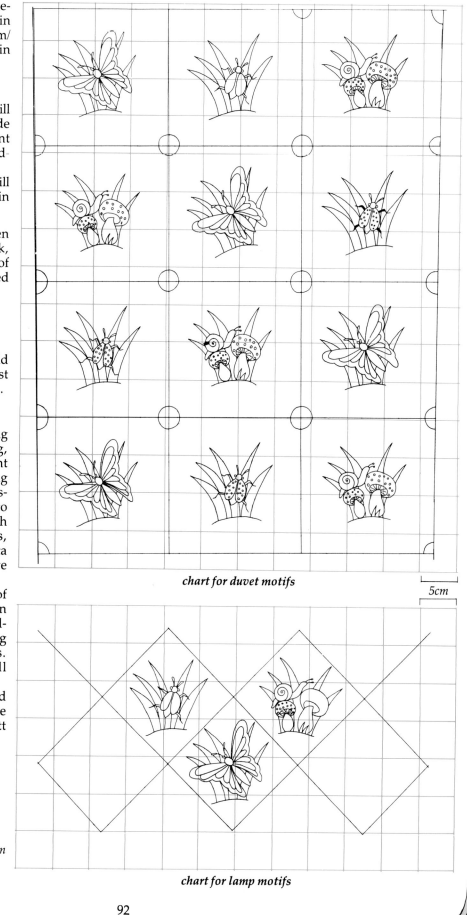

chart for duvet motifs

5cm

chart for lamp motifs

Cot cover and lampshade

The cot cover measures 71cm/28in by 52cm/21in when finished; the lampshade measures 34cm/13½in high by 79cm/31in circumference.

Materials

Fabric: approximately 76cm/30in by 59cm/23in white Pongee 5 mommie for the quilt: 40cm/15½in deep by 84cm/33in wide white Pongee 5 mommie for the lampshade.

Paints: peony red, chrome yellow, golden yellow, orange, cornflower blue, peacock blue, jade green and combinations of all these colours, as well as diluted versions.

Gutta: natural, yellow, black.

Method examples

For the lampshade trace the chair (not the bench) on to the silk.

The paving stones gradually become lighter towards the background. Prepare two saucers of paint: one containing orange, the other golden yellow, both slightly diluted. At each row of paving stones add a bit more water and alcohol to the paints to dilute and lighten the colours.

Leave one side of the balloons lighter to make them appear rounded. The balloon strings are painted in yellow gutta, and the knot holding them together in black gutta.

The flecks on the girl's dress are made by adding light touches of cornflower blue with a fine brush when the paint is nearly dry. Use pale pink shaded with light brown and a mixture of diluted grey and peacock blue for skin tones and black gutta for the girl's eyes.

Opposite: balloons for sale on this beautiful cot cover and matching lampshade.

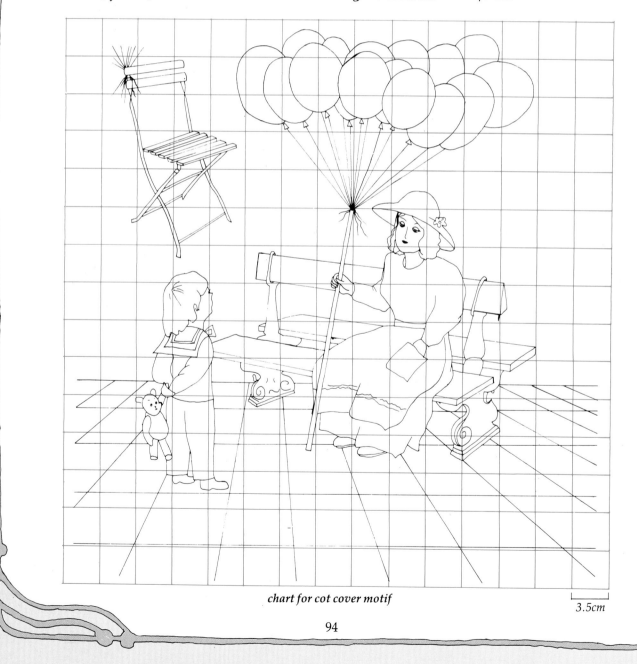

chart for cot cover motif

3.5cm

Index

If you are interested in any other of the art and craft titles published by Search Press
please send for free colour catalogue to:
Search Press Limited, Dept B, Wellwood, North Farm Road, Tunbridge Wells, Kent TN2 3DR